LIFE, ACCORDING TO ME

LIFE, ACCORDING TO ME

To my sweet little kids who spent many nights recording the small details of their day.
You made staying up past bedtime memorable and fun and taught me to
savor those tender moments of motherhood.

Written by Stephanie Dulgarian, www.SomewhatSimple.com
Design by Hayley Castle, www.hayleycastle.com

GOOD MORNING!

TODAY IS

WHEN **I** **wake up** in the *morning,* **I...**

I USUALLY WAKE UP at ___ : ___ A.M.

My *favorite* THING TO EAT FOR breakfast is...

A note TO: _____

_____

_____

_____

_____

_____

FROM, _____

A NOTE to: _____

_____

_____

_____

_____

From, _____

SO SILLY

TODO IS _____

The SILLIEST THING I've ever done IS...

I THINK

IS so silly!

A note TO: _____

_____
_____
_____
_____
_____

FROM, _____

A NOTE to: _____

_____
_____
_____
_____
_____

From, _____

STAY TUNED

TODAY IS

MY *favorite* TV shows **ARE...**

A note TO

FROM,

A NOTE to:

There are _____ TV's **IN** MY house!

I **DO** DO **NOT**

HAVE a TV **IN** MY room.
(circle one)

From,

3

I AM KIND

TODAY IS

THE last time I did SOMETHING
really kind WAS WHEN I...

Tomorrow I WILL TRY
EXTRA hard
to be KIND TO...

A note TO: _____

_____
_____
_____

FROM, _____

A NOTE to: _____

_____
_____
_____

From, _____

4

HAIR DO'S AND DONT'S

TODAY IS

THIS is what my HAIR looks like:

If I COULD have crazy hair FOR one day, I WOULD color it
A. PINK
b. Green
c. Purple Polka Dots
d. OTHER _____

A note TO:

_____
_____
_____
_____
_____
_____
_____

FROM,

A NOTE to:

_____
_____
_____
_____
_____
_____

From,

NICE PEOPLE

TODAY IS

The last REALLY kind **THING** someone DID for me was...

I THINK

is the **nicest** PERSON IN THE world!

A NOTE to:

_____
_____
_____
_____
_____
_____

From,
_____

A note TO:

_____
_____
_____
_____
_____

FROM,
_____

6

SURPRISE!

TODAY IS

THE biggest surprise I HAVE EVER had was...

I wish SOMEONE WOULD surprise ME WITH

a. A NEW PET

B. $50

c. Other

_____

A note TO:

_____

_____

FROM,

A NOTE to:_____

_____

_____

From,

THAT IS OLD!

TODAY IS

The OLDEST **thing I OWN** is...

The oldest PERSON I know IS...

A note TO:

_____
_____
_____
_____
_____
_____
_____
_____

FROM,
_____

A NOTE to:

_____
_____
_____
_____
_____
_____
_____
_____
_____
_____
_____

From,
_____

They are

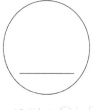

years OLD!

LUNCHTIME

TODAY IS

For lunch TODAY I ATE...

MY favorite thing TO EAT for LUNCH is...

A note TO:

_____

_____

_____

FROM, _____

A NOTE to: _____

_____

_____

_____

From, _____

OOPS!

TODAY IS

Everyone **makes** MISTAKES, HERE IS **one** I MADE:

I

HAVE

or

HAVE NOT

been **IN** a CAR accident.

(circle one)

A note TO:

_____

_____

_____

_____

_____

_____

FROM,

A NOTE to:

_____

_____

_____

_____

_____

_____

From,

SMILE!

Something THAT IS **MAKING**
me happy right NOW IS...

I HAVE

_____

tch IN

MY mouth.

A note TO:

_____
_____
_____
_____
_____
_____
_____

FROM, _____

A NOTE to:

_____
_____
_____
_____
_____
_____

From, _____

11

HOBBIES

TODAY IS

MY favorite
HOBBY is...

I used TO spend
A LOT OF time on
THIS HOBBY:

A note TO: _____

_____
_____
_____
_____
_____

FROM, _____

A NOTE to: _____

_____
_____
_____
_____
_____

From, _____

GET DRESSED

MY FAVORITE thing
to wear IS:

A note TO:

_____

_____
_____
_____
_____
_____
_____
_____

FROM,
_____

Я NOTE to: _____

_____
_____
_____
_____
_____
_____
_____
_____
_____

From,
_____

I DO or DO NOT

HAVE A SCHOOL uniform.

(circle one)

13

SELF PORTRAIT

TODAY IS

This is what I look LIKE right NOW:

My favorite
THING
ABOUT
my body is:

a. MY EYES

B. MY HAIR

c. My smile

d. Other _____

A note TO: _____

_____

_____

FROM, _____

A NOTE to: _____

_____

_____

From, _____

LET'S TALK

5 PEOPLE I talked TO today WERE:

My favorite PERSON to TALK to is...

A note TO:

FROM,

A NOTE to:

From,

FREE TIME

TODAY IS

My FAVORITE things TO DO in my FREE TIME are...

Someday I WANT to LEARN how to...

A NOTE to:

_____
_____
_____
_____
_____
_____

From,
_____

A note TO:

_____
_____
_____
_____
_____

FROM,
_____

16

LET'S BE FRIENDS

TODAY IS

Here **is a** LIST OF MY *friends:*

My BEST friend IS:

A *note* TO:

_____

_____

FROM,

A NOTE to:

_____

_____

From,

MY NEIGHBORHOOD

TODAY IS

HERE IS **A** description of where **MY** HOUSE is:

The best PART **ABOUT** my neighborhood IS...

A note TO:

_____
_____
_____
_____
_____
_____
_____
_____

FROM,

A NOTE to:

_____
_____
_____
_____
_____
_____
_____
_____
_____
_____

From,

MY HOUSE

TODAY IS

HERE is a description OF WHAT my house LOOKS like:

There are

_____

BEDROOMS

IN MY house.

A note TO:

_____
_____
_____
_____

FROM,
_____

A NOTE to

_____
_____
_____
_____
_____
_____

From,
_____

MY ROOM

TODAY IS

Here is a **DESCRIPTION** OF **what my** ROOM looks like:

I share A room WITH...

A note TO:

_____
_____
_____
_____
_____
_____

FROM,

A NOTE to:

_____
_____
_____
_____
_____
_____
_____
_____

From,

EATING OUT

MY **FAVORITE** restaurant is...

Number OF TIMES my FAMILY EATS at a restaurant.

A note TO:

_____ _____
_____
_____
_____
_____
_____
_____

FROM, _____

A NOTE to:

_____ _____
_____
_____
_____
_____
_____

From, _____

MY RIDE

TODAY IS

Here **IS A** description OF THE car(s) my family DRIVES:

MY dream CAR is...

A note TO: _____

_____

_____

_____

_____

_____

FROM, _____

A NOTE to: _____

_____

_____

_____

_____

_____

From, _____

22

THE DAILY GRIND

TODAY IS

HERE is what I
    do EVERY **DAY**:

A note TO:

_____

_____

_____

_____

_____

_____

_____

_____

FROM,

A NOTE to: _____

_____

_____

_____

_____

_____

_____

From,

ONE word to describe MY DAY
TODAY would be:

LOVE

TODAY IS

The PEOPLE **I** LOVE **most** are...

Things I **love:**
(circle all that apply)

BUNNIES

chocolate   babies

BUGS

lollipops

VEGETABLES

sunshine

SHOPPING
swimming

reading

NAPTIME

MOVIES

dancing

A note TO: _____

_____
_____
_____

FROM, _____

A NOTE to: _____

_____
_____
_____

From, _____

THE FUTURE

TODAY IS

One thing **I AM** EXCITED about for the FUTURE is...

I think it WOULD be really NEAT to OWN A:

a. Flying car

b. Time machine

C. SPACESHIP

A note TO:

_____

_____

_____

_____

_____

FROM,

A NOTE to

_____

_____

_____

_____

From,

BOOK SMART

TODAY IS

My FAVORITE and least **FAVORITE** subjects IN school **ARE:**

I THINK

IS THE smartest person IN the WORLD!

A NOTE to:

_____
_____
_____
_____
_____
_____

From,
_____

A note TO:

_____
_____
_____
_____
_____

FROM,
_____

GAME TIME

TODAY IS

HERE is a **list** OF *games* **I** LOVE:

My *favorite* INDOOR GAME is:

MY *favorite* OUTDOOR game is:

A note TO:

_____

_____

_____

FROM,

A NOTE to:

_____

_____

_____

From,

RIGHT NOW

TODAY IS

Right now I
AM FEELING...

RIGHT NOW, I SEE:

I hear:

I SMELL:

A note TO

_____
_____
_____
_____
_____
_____
_____
_____

FROM,

A NOTE to:

_____
_____
_____
_____
_____
_____
_____
_____
_____
_____

From,

VACATION

TODAY IS

THE *best* VACATION **I have ever BEEN** on was...

Someday want TO VISIT

A note TO

_____
_____
_____
_____

FROM,_____

A NOTE to _____

_____
_____
_____
_____
_____

From,_____

FAVORITES

TODAY IS

My FAVORITE thing about TODAY was...

My favorite...

COLOR:

FOOD:

book:

season:

DAY of the WEEK:

A note TO:

_____
_____
_____
_____
_____
_____

FROM, _____

A NOTE to:

_____
_____
_____
_____
_____
_____
_____
_____

From,

YOU'RE JOKING

TODAY IS

Here IS A FUNNY joke
OR something FUNNY that happened:

The funniest
PERSON I
KNOW is...

A note TO:

_____

_____

_____

_____

_____

_____

_____

FROM, _____

A NOTE to:

_____

_____

_____

_____

_____

_____

From, _____

BOO!

TODAY IS

HERE is a time **I GOT REALLY** scared...

I am afraid OF:

A note TO: _____

_____
_____
_____
_____
_____
_____

FROM, _____

A NOTE to: _____

_____
_____
_____
_____
_____
_____

From, _____

GOOD NIGHT!

TODAY IS

BEFORE I go to BED, I...

A note TO:

_____

_____

_____

_____

_____

_____

_____

_____

_____

FROM,

A NOTE to: _____

_____

_____

_____

_____

_____

_____

_____

_____

I usually go to BED AT

_____ : _____ P.M.

From,

I DON'T LIKE IT!

TODAY IS

MY *least* favorite **THING** TO DO **is...**

I don't LIKE EATING:

A note TO: _____

_____

_____

_____

FROM, _____

A NOTE to: _____

_____

_____

_____

From, _____

THE PAST

TODAY IS

If **I** COULD go back IN time, **I'D**...

Something OR SOMEONE I miss:

A note TO:

A NOTE To:

FROM,

From,

GROWING UP

TODAY IS

When I GROW UP,
I want to be...

I AM
going TO have

_____

KIDS someday.

A NOTE to:

_____
_____
_____
_____

From,

A note TO:

_____
_____
_____
_____

FROM,

TIME TO READ

TODAY IS

Let me TELL YOU ABOUT my favorite BOOK:

The LAST BOOK I read was...

A note TO: _____

_____

_____

FROM, _____

A NOTE to: _____

_____

From, _____

LET'S SING

TODAY IS

Let me tell **YOU** about THE MUSIC **I enjoy:**

My favorite SONG IS...

A note TO:

_____
_____
_____
_____
_____
_____
_____

FROM, _____

A NOTE to:

_____
_____
_____
_____
_____
_____
_____
_____
_____

From, _____

OUCH!

TODAY IS

HERE is a **time I** GOT REALLY hurt:

I have OR have not had STITCHES.

A note TO:

_____
_____
_____
_____

FROM,
_____

A NOTE to: _____

_____
_____
_____
_____
_____
_____

From,
_____

SCHOOL DAYS

TODAY IS

HERE is what the FIRST DAY of school WAS LIKE FOR me:

My teacher's NAME IS...

I am IN

grade.

A note TO:

_____
_____
_____
_____
_____
_____

FROM,

A NOTE to:

_____
_____
_____
_____
_____
_____
_____
_____

From,

SHOW ME THE MONEY

TODAY IS

The CHORES AND JOBS I do TO earn money ARE...

IF I had a MILLION dollars, I would...

A note TO:

_____

_____
_____
_____
_____
_____
_____
_____

FROM, _____

A NOTE to:

_____

_____
_____
_____
_____
_____
_____
_____

From, _____

www.SomewhatSimple.com

THE BEST DAY

TODAY IS

LET me **TELL YOU** about THE BEST day **OF** my life:

Right NOW, I feel...

A note TO: _____

_____

_____

_____

_____

_____

_____

FROM, _____

A NOTE to: _____

_____

_____

_____

_____

_____

From, _____

MY FAMILY

Let ME tell you ABOUT MY FAMILY:

A note TO _____

_____
_____
_____
_____
_____
_____
_____

FROM, _____

A NOTE to _____

_____
_____
_____
_____
_____
_____
_____
_____

From, _____

I have ___ COUSINS.

I HAVE ___ Aunts.

I have ___ UNCLES.

GOALS

TODAY IS

Here **IS A** LIST of goals I HAVE set:

SOMETHING I'd **LIKE** to do...

Today:

TOMORROW:

THIS WEEK:

This month:

THIS YEAR:

A note TO: _____

_____

_____

_____

FROM,

A NOTE to:

_____

_____

_____

From,

ANIMALS

TODAY IS

Here are all **THE** PETS **MY** family HAS had:

If I could BE ANY animal, **I'D** be a...

A note TO:

_____
_____
_____
_____
_____
_____

FROM,

A NOTE to:

_____
_____
_____
_____
_____
_____

From,
_____

IT'S A TRADITION

TODAY IS

MY FAVORITE *family tradition* **IS...**

My favorite HOLIDAY IS...

𝓐 note TO:

_____

_____

_____

_____

_____

FROM,

_____

𝓐 NOTE to:

_____

_____

_____

_____

_____

From,

_____

I AM SPECIAL

TODAY IS

Let **ME** tell you SOMETHING **I** am really good AT:

HERE is a LIST of MY nicknames:

A note TO: _____

FROM,

A NOTE to: _____

From,

ALMOST FAMOUS

TODAY IS

I'd **LOVE**
TO meet

_____

someday **because...**

The MOST
famous person
I'VE
met IS...

A note TO:

_____
_____
_____
_____
_____
_____

FROM,

A NOTE to:

_____
_____
_____
_____
_____
_____
_____
_____

From,

www.SomewhatSimple.com

HIDDEN TALENT

TODAY IS

SOMETHING most people DON'T know about me is...

IF I could HAVE ONE super power, IT WOULD be

A note TO

_____
_____
_____
_____

FROM,
_____

A NOTE to: _____

_____
_____
_____
_____
_____

From,

MAKE 'EM PROUD

TODAY IS

Let ME TELL YOU about A TIME I won a SPECIAL award:

MY biggest accomplishment IS...

A note TO:

_____
_____
_____
_____
_____
_____

FROM,

A NOTE to:

_____
_____
_____
_____
_____
_____
_____

From,

Stephanie Dulgarian is married to her best friend and together they are raising four kids (with one on the way!) who keep them busy but make life fun! They are California transplants who have been living in Arizona since 2005 and they love living close to family and good friends.

In addition to her duties as a mom and wife, Stephanie is also the author of the creative blog www.SomewhatSimple.com. She is a former preschool teacher and is usually knee-deep in a project. She loves to create, cook, shop, and travel with her family.

Stephanie can be found on the following social media outlets:
Facebook: www.facebook.com/SomewhatSimpleBlog
Twitter: @SimpleStephD
Pinterest: www.pinterest.com/SomewhatSimple/
Google+: search Stephanie Dulgarian
Instagram: www.instagram.com/simplestephd

CPSIA information can be obtained at www.ICGtesting.com
Printed in the USA
BVIW12n1326060417
480537BV00006B/14